Major Incident Management for IT Operations

(2nd Edition)

By Chris Skelton

Sacrifices of a family with a husband and father who is a Major Incident Manager are many.

This book is dedicated to my ever patient and loving family:

Estelle, Connor and Elysia.

Preface

There are numerous books on incident management from different best practices, but few that provide a comprehensive guide to major incident management for information technology IT. Major incident management has become a career choice as many businesses employ specialists responsible for returning services to normal as soon as possible after a major incident while minimising impact to the business. Hence, this book has been written focusing on those elements of major incident management which were not covered in this level of detail by best practice frameworks or by other authors. This book has been written considering the challenges faced by Major Incident Managers focusing on the definition and establishment of a major incident management process, roles, and responsibilities, showing value through matrices and people management during a major incident.

This second edition of the book adds additional value with updates on major incident management tools available, leadership and conflict management, and more information on management during the major incident.

All aspects of major incident management:

1. Introduction to Major Incident Management – A high level introduction discussing what a major incident is and what major incident management is not.

2. Defining What Constitutes a Major Incident – Rules for assigning priorities to incidents, including the definition of what constitutes a major incident as agreed between IT and the business. It outlines sequential steps which could help define which incidents should trigger the invocation of the major incident process.

3. Define Interfaces with Other Functions – Defines the relationship with all stakeholders to build the cross-functional teams.

4. Defining the Engagement and Escalation Plan – Processes that need to be in place to ensure rapid engagement when a major incident is reported.

5. Major Incident Management Tools and Infrastructure – These will enable efficient, effective, and rapid resolution of major incidents.

6. Defining the Major Incident Management Process – The sequence of steps that should occur following a major incident being reported. This includes process flow charts and the definition of roles and responsibilities.

7. Roles and Responsibilities – Agreed and defined responsibilities for all the cross-functional major incident management team members.

8. Communication Plan – Defined and agreed plan to communicate a major incidents status across all stakeholders, to enable continuous service improvement and handover to problem management.

9. SLA's, OLA's and UC's – Defining and agreeing the major incident management service level agreements with the business and the operating level agreements and third-party underpinning contracts required to support these agreements.

10. Major Incident Management Matrix – Measuring performance against service level agreements and key performance indicators.

11. During the Major Incident (Management and Leadership): Tips and tricks for the Major Incident Manager to manage the incident as effectively and efficiently as possible in stressful scenarios.

12. Post Major Incident Review – Identify lessons learnt to enable continuous service improvement and handover to problem management.

13. Succeeding as a Major Incident Manager – Tips and tricks for the Major Incident Manager to manage the incident as effectively and efficiently as possible in stressful scenarios.

Section 1: Introduction

1 Introduction

In this section major incident management will be defined at a fundamental level. It explains the principles of classifying an incident as a major incident and major incident management's place in the incident management lifecycle.

1.1   What is a Major Incident?

Before defining a major incident, we need to define an incident. ITIL defines an incident as:

"An unplanned interruption to an IT Service or reduction in the quality of an IT service."

This definition encompasses all IT incidents irrespective if severity. To define a major incident is more difficult as "major" is subjective. ITIL defines a major incident as:

"The highest category of impact for an incident. A major incident results in significant disruption to the business."

So how much disruption is required before it is a major incident? **The answer is simply that the**

business and IT agree what constitutes a major incident. We would typically know an IT major incident when we see it. Examples could be a high number of impacted users or depriving the business on one or more crucial services. With different service level agreement (SLA) parameters across businesses/organisations each will decide which priority incidents will be categorised as major incidents to meet their unique requirements. This is usually defined by an agreed impact/urgency matrix. Incident classification will be explained in more detail in Section 2.

Another definition to be aware of is a "crisis." A crisis is a major incident but with the added element of being a threat to the organisation as a whole. An example could be a catastrophic and persistent network outage impacting the entire organisation's ability to function.

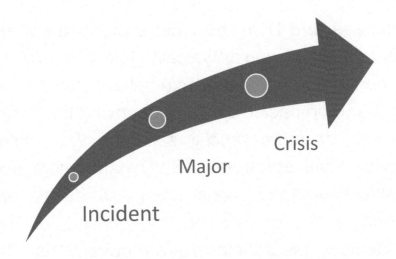

Figure 1: Focus on major incident.

1.2   What is Major Incident Management?

The purpose of the incident management process is to restore normal service operation as quickly as possible and minimize the adverse impact on business operations, ensuring that agreed levels of service quality are maintained. If an event has significant impact or urgency for the business/organisation it demands a response beyond the routine incident management process. When an incident is defined as a major incident normal incident management procedure are abandoned and major incident management procedures are invoked. Major incident management procedures have an emphasis on urgent response, communications with all stakeholders and resource engagement, deployment, and coordination.

A major incident procedure should establish a dedicated major incident team led by a Major Incident Manager. This team will concentrate on the incident alone and ensure that adequate resources are provided to finding a resolution as quickly as possible.

Major incident management may differ from crisis management in that a crisis requires a response beyond the major incident management process. This would include strategic issues such as managing media relations and shareholder confidence, and when to invoke business continuity plans. Large complex organisations will have a crisis management strategy, model and plan that augments major incident management. In other organisations the major incident process will suffice. The quantifiable differences between a crisis and a major incident in large complex organisations is the scope of impact and complexity.

Incident Management		
Management of low to medium impact incidents.	**Major Incident Management**	
	Incidents with significant impact or urgency for the business / organisation demanding a response beyond the routine incident management process.	**Crisis Management**
		A major incident with the added element of being a threat to the organisation as a whole. Includes strategic issues such as managing media relations, shareholders confidence and when to invoke business contingency plans.

Figure 2: The overlap between incident management, major incident management and crisis management.

1.3 What Major Incident Management is not?

Major incident management focuses only on the subset of incidents defined as "major." **What constitutes a major incident is agreed between**

the business and IT. It is not problem management, it is not root cause analysis, it is not change management and it is not finding a permanent solution. These are all separate processes. Incident management is restoring services as quickly as possible which may include a temporary workaround. Major incident management has the same objective as incident management, but the skillsets are different.

Section 2: Defining a Major Incident

2 Defining What Constitutes a Major Incident

Rules need to be defined for assigning priorities to incidents, including the definition of what constitutes a major incident. The following sequential steps could help define which incidents should trigger the invocation of the major incident process.

Figure 3: Steps to define what constitutes a major incident

2.1 Review of Service Level Agreements and Service Catalogues

Working with the Business Relationship Manager and business representatives determine the mission critical services and components. This will define which services, when impacted by an incident, could invoke the major incident management process. One of the ways to do this would be to categorise services based on their criticality:

Service Category	A	B	C	D
Applicability	Vital business functions / Core shared infrastructure	Important Business functions / Vital support functions	Medium production systems	Occasional use or low priority support systems
Criticality	Mission Critical	Critical	Important	Low
Service Availability Service Level Agreement	Business – 99% Infrastructure – 99.5%	99%	98.5%	95%

Table 1: Service categories

This is a first pass on defining which categories of services may require the major incident management process to be invoked for high severity incidents. This can initially be drafted by holding brainstorming sessions among the relevant support groups, service desk supervisors, incident and problem managers, and business representatives. These sessions can be repeated on periodic review to ensure that they remain relevant. In this example IT and the business may agree that category C and D incidents could not by definition of their criticality be of a severity that would invoke a major incident management process.

The organisation may have subcategories. There may be a select few services in category A that are as marked as "franchise risk" (or any other appropriate name). Examples of these services could be the primary customer facing front end system of a corporate bank used to initiate all transactions or an airports core system that receives and routes flight information and schedules. Any disruption of these services would have the severest of impacts to the business.

This is a useful exercise before defining incident priorities as it limits the justifiable invocation of the major incident management process to the critical services.

2.2   Define Categories of Urgency

The definitions of categories of urgency will be unique to each organisation. Each organisation will have multiple urgency scenarios. The following table provides examples of one potential urgency scenario by organisation type. When determining an incident's urgency, the highest relevant category is chosen:

Category	Urgency Scenario Description
High	**Financial bank**: Highly time sensitive transaction processing cannot be completed **Airport:** IT baggage transfer application failure with flight due to depart within the next two hours at risk of cancellation. **Internet service provider**: Considerable number of customers have lost their internet connectivity. **Any:** Systems have been hacked or infected by a virus impacting multiple users with a risk of spreading.
Medium	**Financial bank:** Transaction processing delayed with country clearing house cut off 8 or more hours away. **Airport**: IT baggage transfer application degraded performance with flight due to depart in more than two less than eight hours away at risk of cancellation.
Low	**Financial bank**: System providing monthly volume reports to the central bank failing with report delivery deadline one week away. **Airport**: Degraded performance of baggage transfer application with ten passengers booked on flights at risk of having their baggage delivered on a later flight.

Table 2: Categories of urgency

2.3 Define Categories of Impact

As with urgency, the definitions of categories of impact will be unique to each organisation. The following table provides examples of one potential impact scenario by organisation type. When determining an incident's impact, the highest relevant category is chosen:

Category	Impact Scenario Description
High	**Financial bank:** Value of transactions missing clearing cut off exceeds £1,000,000. **Airport**: Flights cancelled or delayed by more than 1 hour. Internet service provider: Considerable number of customers have lost their internet connectivity. **Any:** Systems have been hacked or infected by a virus impacting multiple users preventing or contaminating time sensitive work and data security at risk.
Medium	**Financial bank**: Value of transactions missing clearing cut off exceeds $100 000 but is less than $1,000,000. **Airport:** Flights delayed by under one hour.
Low	**Financial bank:** Value of transactions missing clearing cut off is less than $100 000. **Airport:** Only ten passengers will have their baggage delivered on later flights.

Table 3: Categories of impact

2.4   Define Priority Classes

Incident priority is derived from urgency and impact by an incident priority matrix:

		Impact		
		High	Medium	Low
Urgency	High	Priority 1	Priority 2	Priority 3
	Medium	Priority 2	Priority 3	Priority 4
	Low	Priority 3	Priority 4	Priority 5

Table 4: Incident priority matrix

Now in agreement with the business target response time and target resolution times can be defined for each priority class:

Priority	Description	Target Response Time	Target Resolution Time
Priority 1	Critical	15 minutes	2 hours
Priority 2	High	30 minutes	4 hours
Priority 3	Medium	1 hour	8 hours
Priority 4	Low	4 hours	24 hours
Priority 5	Cosmetic	1 Day	1 week

Table 5: Priority classes

2.5   Define Major Incident by Service (Scenario Routing Matrix)

With priority classes defined we can now define circumstances that will warrant an incident to be treated as a major incident. To do this a scenario routing matrix can be produced by the IT and business owners of each service. Let us use an example of an organisation that provides and supports a digital two-way radio network that is a category A service:

Scenario	Priority	Routing	Business Communication	Major Incident?	Crisis?
Catastrophic failure: Radio user are not able to communicate via radio on all sites	Priority 1 24x7x365	Digital Radio Support	Yes	Yes 24x7x365	Yes
Localised failure: Radio users at a single site not able to communicate via radio	Priority 2 24x7x365	Digital Radio Support	Yes	Yes 24x7x365	No
Services and features such as voice recording, Client terminals, data services fail	Priority 3 24x7x365	Digital Radio Support	Yes	No	No
Radio user would not notice impact to radio environment.	Priority 4	Digital Radio Support	No	No	No

Table 6: Scenario routing matrix example

This scenario routing matrix provides a service desk analyst with a simple easy to follow guide to define the priority of the incident and engage the right processes.

2.6   Prioritization Exceptions

As with most rules there are exceptions. Exceptions are:

- Having established the rules that define what constitutes a major incident the real world can still outflank you. Where there is an incident scenario that proves to be a "grey" area it is important to define the authority to determine if it is a major incident.

- Some scenarios may be considered a major incident temporarily. For example, if a service is continually unstable and the decision is made to provide enhanced support, then additional scenarios may temporarily constitute a major incident until stability is achieved.

- Another example would be where a key client is dissatisfied and at risk requiring additional scenarios impacting that client to temporarily constitute a major incident.

2.7 Finalise Major Incident Management Scope with the Business

Let us now summarise the agreement between the business and IT on when the major incident management process will be invoked:

- Priority classes have been defined and major incident management will be invoked when an incident is categorised as a priority 1 or priority 2 incident.
- Authorities have been defined to declare an incident as a major incident where the priority is difficult to define.
- The services that are in scope for major incident management based on their criticality are defined. "Table1: Service Categories" can be expanded to define the highest priority ticket that each category can generate:

Service Category	A	B	C	D
Applicability	Vital business functions / Core shared infrastructure	Important Business functions / Vital support functions	Medium production systems	Occasional use or low priority support systems
Criticality	Mission Critical	Critical	Important	Low
Service Availability SLA	Business – 99% Infrastructure – 99.5%	99%	98.5%	95%
Highest Possible Priority Incident	Priority 1	Priority 2	Priority 3	Priority 4

Table 7: Finalised major incident scope

- Temporary exceptions for services or customers "in distress" can be agreed as they occur.
- Periodic reviews are agreed to ensure the service categories remain relevant.

Section 3: Define Interfaces with Other Functions

3 Define Interfaces with Other Functions

Effective and efficient major incident management would require the establishment of a team with membership engaged across the organisation. When defining a major incident management process all stakeholders should be identified with responsibilities, communication channels and escalation procedures agreed. Typical stakeholders would include:

3.1 Service Desk

In most organisations the service desk is the single point of contact between the IT services being provided and the users. If an event has significant impact or urgency for the business/organisation it demands a response beyond the routine incident management process the major incident management process is invoked. The service desk, be it local, centralised, virtual, follow the sun, or a specialised service desk group, needs to be familiar with the definition of a major incident as agreed with the business and invoke the major incident management process when appropriate. The handover process and any residual responsibilities maintained by the service desk during a major incident should be agreed and documented.

3.2 Business Relationship Management

Major incident management provides value to the business by resolving major incidents to minimize impact to the clients. Major incidents are highly visible to the business and is therefore relatively easy to demonstrate its value. Major incident management aligns incident resolution to real-time business priorities.

3.3 Crisis Management

A crisis is a major incident but with the added element of being a threat to the organisation. An example could be a catastrophic and persistent network outage impacting the entire organisation's ability to function. Many corporations may have a defined crisis management process. This crisis management process should define the major incident management interface.

3.4   Change Management

The major incident management process will need to resolve incidents resulting from failed changes. Investigative analysis of recent changes to impacted components is typically one of the first priorities when the root cause is not known. Additionally, a change may be required to implement a workaround or resolution. This will need to be logged as a request for change (RFC) and progressed through the change management process. The process and approval authorities for emergency changes to urgently minimise the impact of a major incident should be documented.

3.5 IT Service Continuity Management (ITSCM)

Organisations may have a business continuity plan (BCP). Business continuity planning is the creation of a strategy through the recognition of threats and risks facing a company, with an eye to ensure that personnel and assets are protected and able to function in the event of a disaster. Business continuity management (BCM) provides initial business Impact and risk analysis activities. IT is just one service that the business relies on, and IT Service Continuity Management (ITSCM) supports the BCP by producing a supporting ITSCM strategy. It supports the overall BCM process by ensuring that the required IT technical and services facilities (including computer systems, networks, applications, telecommunications, technical support, and service desk) can be recovered within required, and agreed, business timescales for organisation. Where there is no BCP then ITSCM would typically perform all these activities. Figure 2 showing the overlap between incident management, major incident management and crisis management can now be extended to show the overlap between ITSCM as part of BCM.

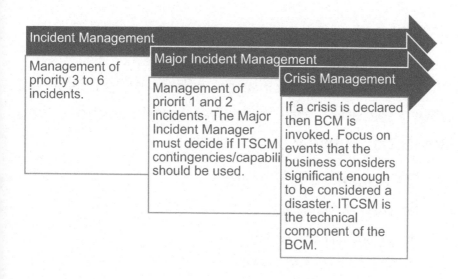

Figure 4: ITSCM as part of BCM

The major incident management alignment with ITSCM and BCM needs to be clearing defined. The pre-conditions that constitute a disaster need to be defined as part of the ITSCM process. A documented strategy for recovering the IT infrastructure or IT business application after a disaster needs to be in place. Guidance will need to be provided to other areas of the business and IT on continuity and recovery related issues.

3.6 Resolution Management

A Major Incident Manager relies on IT subject matter experts for technical workarounds and resolutions. These would include:

- Database administrators
- System administrators
- Application support
- Infrastructure support
- Network support
- Information security
- Access management
- Cloud, Wi-Fi, engineering, and other technology resources

Resolution teams may be third party vendors. IT operations including major incident management to ensure the vendor underpinning contracts and operating level agreements are aligned with the major incident process service level agreements. The contracts should specify engagement processes and timelines. Each vendor will have unique support contracts. Some may agree join a conference line for the duration of a major incident while others will only provide high level updates published on their website. The Major Incident Manager will need to understand the agreements with each vendor and manage stakeholder expectations accordingly.

Additionally, Major Incident Managers will need to engage business and operations resources to manage the incident impact for its duration and after the technology incident is resolved.

Pre-defined engagement processes and communication channels should be in place with all stakeholders.

3.7　Service Asset and Configuration Management

The configuration management system (CMS) provides the service desk with the information required to categorise the incident and determine if the major incident management process should be invoked. It is used by the Major Incident Manager and the resolution teams to identify faulty equipment and to assess the impact of an incident. A detailed and accurate configuration management database (CMDB) simplifies and accelerates the investigation and resolution process.

3.8　Capacity Management

Capacity management may develop workarounds for major incidents and help in managing any capacity issues caused by the incident.

3.9   Availability Management

Availability management uses incident management data to determine the availability of IT services and investigate where incident lifecycles can be improved. Expected impact on availability is a factor in defining the priority of an incident.

3.10 Service Level Management (SLM)

A key part of major incident management delivering to an agreed level of service is the ability to resolve incidents in a specified time. Major incident management enables SLM to define measurable responses to major service disruptions. SLM defines the required levels of service within which major incident management works. This will include:

- Major incident management engagement and response times
- Impact definitions
- Target fix times
- User and other stakeholders feedback expectations

3.11 Corporate Communications

When the impact of the major incident is visible to patrons, customers and third parties it is important to ensure communications with the extended world is managed. More about this in Section 8: Major Incident Communications Plan.

3.12 Problem Management

Incident management is about restoring services as quickly as possible which may include a temporary workaround. Problem management investigates and resolves the underlying cause to prevent or reduce the impact of recurrence. The handover process should be in place for problem management to take ownership of the root cause analysis and fix implementation.

3.13 Defining Major Incident Management Interfaces in a Service Integration and Management (SIAM) Model

SIAM focuses on managing the delivery of services provided by multiple suppliers. SIAM is a service capability and set of practices in a model and approach that combines the benefits of best-of-breed based multi-sourcing of services with the simplicity of single sourcing, minimising the risks inherent in multi-sourced approaches and masking the supply chain complexity from the consumers of the services. SIAM assists in the situation where policy and execution can no longer be defined absolutely by a single authority, supporting the development of supply chains into supply networks.

Some SIAM models also include a centralised service desk and incident management function. Standards for exchanging incident management information must be defined. Where possible, suppliers should be encouraged to adopt your organisations major incident management standards and processes. If this is not SIAM will need to be competent in translating and managing multiple major incident management standards.

It is unlikely that a SIAM will get a provider of a commodity service that is used by thousands of customers worldwide to adopt its definition of incident severities. The incident management process will still need consistency by mapping the provider's severity levels to its own.

Relationships with suppliers can be the responsibility of the service level manager or owned by process owners with peer-to-peer relationships across the partner organisations. While this relationship is important, the experience is that SIAM is most effective when relationships are also built between ITIL process owner peers across the different organisations. This supports joint development of interface standards, such as common minimum incident datasets, and supports the resolution of issues with process capability and maturity.

Challenges to be addressed when implementing a major incident management function within a SIAM model include:

- Development of common severity level definitions and what constitutes a major incident.
- Development of an effective incident management policy.
- Development of incident management toolset integration standards between suppliers.
- Development and improvement of key performance indicators.
- Development of benchmarking approaches for capability and maturity assessment and improvement. For example, where the SIAM and suppliers have different toolsets:
  - Do all parties use the same severity definitions?
  - What if the SIAM uses severity 1 to 6, with 1 the highest, but the supplier uses 4 to 1 with 4 the highest?
  - What method does each provider's tool use if a 'resolved' incident is not resolved?
  - Do they allow an incident to be re-opened, or does a new one need to be created?

- Clear ownership of major incidents and problems where the causing supplier is unclear.

SIAM implementation must initially focus on capturing and sharing relevant incident and restoration information across all suppliers, to prevent re-occurrence irrespective of which service was initially affected. Considering all suppliers to be part of the same enterprise.

Section 4:

Define the Engagement and Escalation Plan

4 Define the Engagement and Escalation Plan

What constitutes a major incident has been defined. The major incident management team participants and stakeholders have been identified and the interface with each of them defined. To ensure rapid engagement and ongoing engagement a contact list, availability roster and escalation plan by service should be defined and collated. Each of these should be available in the IT service management knowledge base with access provided to appropriate resources. These are crucial elements that will help a Major Incident Manager quickly engage all participants as soon as possible when a major incident is declared.

4.1 Contact List

The contact list should capture names, job titles, telephone numbers, e-mail addresses and methods of communication of various individual team members and third-party suppliers involved in the major incident process. Applicable contact details should also be published in any published scenario routing matrices.

4.2   Availability Roster

An availability roster should be in place ensuring coverage both in and out of office hours. This roster should include coverage when key resources as out of office. An alternative is to have a single number that will forward any calls to the appropriate available resource.

4.3   The Escalation Plan

Escalation is a formal process to highlight the issue at hand to a higher authority. For example, if a certain team member is not willing to or is not able to do a certain activity, he or she is responsible for, it is necessary to escalate the issue to the superior for resolution. A team member's questionable capability to address an issue, resource and inter-group conflicts, a major incident resolution exceeding the SLA, and a senior management decision required to invoke ITSCM are known situations calling for escalations. These issues may require higher level intervention because the authority, decision making, resources or effort required to resolve them are beyond a Major Incident Manager's horizon. At times, the Major Incident Manager may want to involve higher authorities for information-only escalations to keep them abreast of potential issues managing the incident.

Rules of engagement need to be defined for the Major Incident Manager to escalate issues up the internal and third-party management hierarchies when appropriate. The escalation plan provides a hierarchy of names, job titles and telephone numbers. It will contain rules guiding the Major Incident Manager on when to invoke an escalation.

Section 5:

Major Incident Management Tools and Infrastructure

5 Major Incident Management Tools and Infrastructure

5.1　IT Service Management Software

When your information is spread over ticketing systems, emails, spreadsheets, and basic desktop management tools, management is challenging for all IT functions including major incident management. It is difficult to create end-to-end processes and you cannot get the visibility you need to respond efficiently and accurately to your business. An integrated IT toolset will enable the Major Incident Manager by providing the following:

5.1.1 Workflow or Process Control Software

Workflow and process control software provides the documentation of defined processes - along with roles and responsibilities that will achieve the desired outcomes. In addition to the major incident team the technical resolver and service management teams should have access to the documented major incident process.

5.1.2 Central Service Management Tool

This tool centralises all activities within the IT operation. It is vital in connecting the entire operation with the business. For major incidents, an incident ticket is logged (or upgraded to a major incident when it is identified. This provides a pivotal point of information for stakeholders, Additionally, it provides a basis for post incident review, detailing the chronology of the major incident. In addition to incident and major incident workflow management functionality the following functionality would be embedded in the central service management tool:

- Incident management system with a ticketing tool that engages users and other stakeholders and can manage all processes that surround major incidents – improving visibility and control. The system will prioritise incidents based on business impact and urgency and drives them through the entire resolution process.

- Change workflow management enabling the major incident process to quickly identify and review changes applied to the impacted component(s).

- Problem management functionality enabling the association of problems with incidents.

- Configuration management database (CMDB) - An integrated configuration management database with relationships defined that enables evaluation of upstream and downstream impact when a specific component fails

- Known error database (KEDB): is a database that describes all the known issues within the overall system. It describes the situations in which these issues appear, and when possible, it offers workaround that will restore services.

5.1.3 Web Portals and Status Pages

These keep stakeholders aware of service outages in real-time. These simplify the information pertinent to end users to keep them aware of the service status.

5.1.4 Telephones

With distinct parts of the organisation involved in major incident resolution phones are vital and should include functionality for pre-programming common numbers, headset, microphone, and conference call capability.

5.1.5 Intelligent Voice Recognition (IVR)

These guide callers to the right function or provide automated support instructions. They can be used to announce service outages and request specific actions during a major incident.

5.1.6 Wars rooms / Command Centres

These are dedicated rooms where the major incident resolvers can congregate with whiteboards, conference facilities, power points and speaker phones all readily available. Where the stakeholders all spread across multiple locations the room is extended into a virtual war room using the available collaboration tools.

5.1.7 Event Monitoring and Alerting Tools

These provide a comprehensive view of the entire infrastructure enabling the resolving teams to monitor and respond to alerts, analyse, and troubleshoot. Critical alerts could instruct the recipient to engage a Major Incident Manager.

5.1.8 Major Incident Response and Orchestration Tools

These tools simplify major incident management, increase the speed of mobilisation and communication, and consequently reduce downtime. Some service management tools do have built in functionality for managing major incident workflows. Comprehensive major incident response and orchestration tools available are separate tools that will integrate with leading service management platforms.

5.1.9 Chat Realtime Messenger Tools

These allow teams to communicate and collaborate. It is useful when information needs to be transmitted in text format. Advanced offerings can integrate with service management tools and major incident response and orchestration tools.

Communication Infrastructure

The ITSM software incident management ticketing system would be your primary means of communicating major incident management status to all subscribed stakeholders unless augmented by a response and orchestration tool. In addition to e-mail SMS tools are available to establish groups to which updates can be sent or team members can be engaged. It is a good idea to have dedicated published telephone conference lines for major incidents. Collaboration tools should be in place so stakeholders can share information and work together to resolve challenging incidents.

Section 6: Define the Major Incident Process

6 Define the Major Incident Process

Defining the sequential process, is invaluable to ensure an agreed and consistent approach to managing all major incidents.

A major incident process flow chart defines the high-level process with the sequence of action to be taken for all major incidents. The following is only a simple example as each organisation will have unique processes and circumstances.

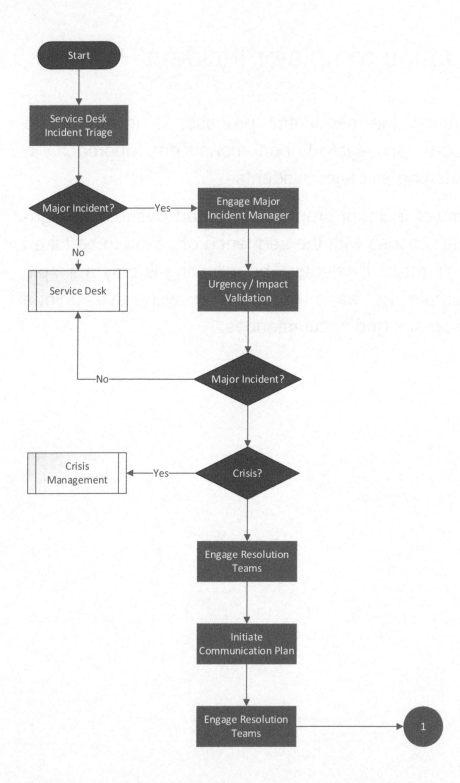

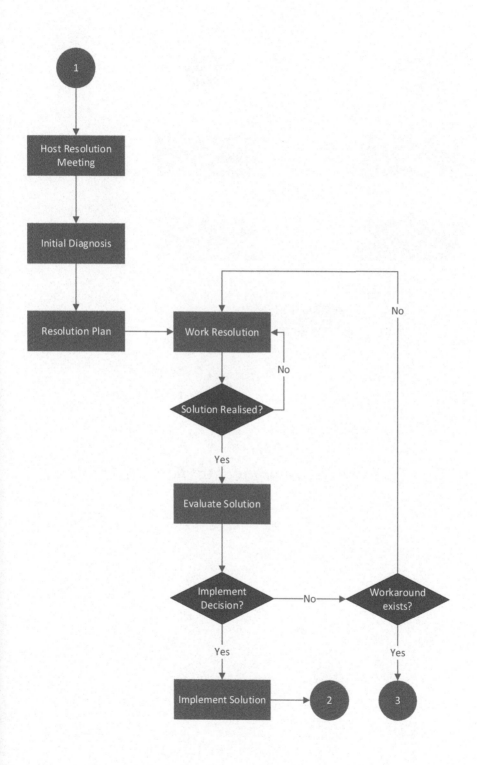

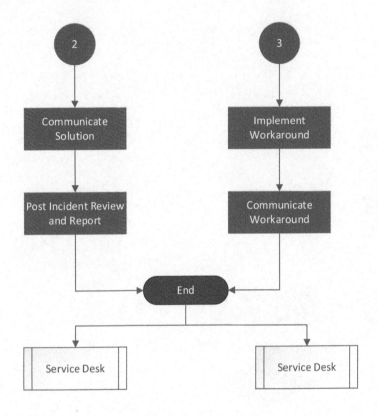

Figure 5: Sample major incident flow process chart

Section 7:

Roles and Responsibilities

7 Roles and Responsibilities

Responsibilities of all major incident stakeholders need to be defined and agreed. There should be no accountability doubt or ambiguity during a major incident. One way to do this is through a RASCI matrix.

The RASCI Matrix assigns and displays responsibilities of individuals or teams during a major incident. RASCI is an acronym from the initial letters of words:

R - Responsible - who is responsible for conducting the task?

A - Accountable - who is responsible for the task and who is responsible for what has been done?

S - Support - who provides support during the implementation of the activity?

C - Consulted - who can provide valuable advice or consultation for the task?

I - Informed - who should be informed about the task progress or the decisions in the task?

RASCI matrix is used for the allocation and assignment of responsibilities to the major incident team members. Use the letters R A S C I in the matrix to describe level of responsibility. There is a rule applied that the overall responsibility (A - Accountability) is the only one person. The people involved (R - Responsibility) should be adequate to the task. Like the flow process chart each organisation will have its unique processes. The following is a simple example:

Activity	Service User	Service Desk	Major Incident Manager	Resolution Teams	Business
Report issue to Service Desk specifying urgency and impact	R/A	C			
Triage incident and establish priority		R/A			
Engage the major incident manager	I	R/A	I/S		
Impact / urgency validation	C	S	R/A		
If appropriate engage crisis management			R/A		
Initiate and continue the communication plan			R/A	S	I
Engage resolution teams			R/A	I	I
Join conference call / or locate to war room	I	I	R/A	R	R
Host technology resolution meeting			R/A	S	I
Complete initial technology diagnosis			R/A	R	S
Complete resolution plan			R/A	R	S/I
Work technology resolution			A	R	
Evaluate technology solution			R/A	R	C
Technology solution decision			R/A	C	I
Implement technology solution	I		A	R	I
If required, implement technology workaround	I		A	R	I
If required, implement business workaround	I		A	I	R
Host post major incident review			R/A	S	S

Table 8: Sample RASCI chart.

Section 8: Communication Plan

8 Communication Plan

8.1 Stakeholder Communications

Maintaining clear communications between all stakeholders is critical during a major incident. The communication plan should describe who needs to know what, how, and how often – from customers to internal staff.

The Major Incident Manager may be accountable for executing the communication plan. In some organisations a dedicated communication manager may be responsible for communications to executives, users, clients external to the organisation and other stakeholders.

The best methods of communications vary by audience and depends primarily on three factors: rapidity of updates, number of message recipients, and confidentiality of data being shared. The following is only a simple example as each organisation will have unique processes and circumstances.

Communication	Distribution	Frequency	Responsible	Method
Major Incident Manager engagement	Major Incident Manager	Once – on declaring a major incident	Service desk manager	Mobile / office / home telephone numbers
Updates to users reporting the issue	All users raising tickets due to the incident	Incident tickets updates at least every hour or as otherwise agreed	Major Incident Manager	Parent incident ticket updates. Automated updates of child tickets
Initial resolution team's engagement	Resolution team members	Once – on declaring a major incident	Major Incident Manager	SMS and email include conference line details
Resolution team members confirm engagement	Major Incident Manager	Once - Within 30 minutes of receiving SMS / email	Resolution team members	Respond to SMS and/or email, join conference call or enter war room
Resolution team engagement follow up	Resolution team members	Until resolution team members or their secondary are engaged	Major Incident Manager	Office / Home / mobile telephone numbers
Awareness alert IT senior management of major incident	Senior IT managers	On major incident declaration / on major incident	Major Incident Manager	Chat group

Communication	Distribution	Frequency	Responsible	Method
		resolution / on queries from senior management		
Updates to the impacted business community	Impacted business management	Priority 1 incident: every hour minutes unless otherwise agreed / Priority 2 incident: every two hours unless otherwise agreed	Major Incident Manager	Mass SMS group
Impacted external customers	Impacted external customers	Defined by the business based on the scenario	Communications Manager	Facebook / LinkedIn / company website / public address system
SLA breach	IT senior management, service owner, Impacted business, communications manager	On SLA breach	Major Incident Manager	e-mail / chat group

Table 9: Sample communication plan template.

8.2   Corporate Communications

A major incident manager is typically responsible for managing communications with internal stakeholders and the customer(s) directly impacted. Visibility of the major incident could extend to the patron population, the press, elected officials, regulators, and other customers. Additionally, the issue may have been shared on social media. Corporate communication engagement should be engaged to manage communications with interested parties.

Additionally, a major incident visible to the world infers a failure of the organisation to provide a reliable service. A well-managed major incident with managed communications can demonstrate the robustness of   the organisations processes in restoring the service.

Section 9:
SLA's OLA's
and UC's

9 SLA's, OLA's and UC's

9.1 Service Level Agreement (SLA)

A service-level agreement is defined as an official commitment that prevails between a service provider and a client. For a major incident management process perspective, the key SLA with the business is the maximum time to resolve an incident. Typically, the higher the incidents priority the shorter the SLA period. The SLA may also define escalation procedures of major incidents based on the incident priority.

9.2 Operational-Level Agreement (OLA)

An operational-level agreement defines the interdependent relationships in support of a service-level agreement. The agreement describes the responsibilities of each internal support group toward other support groups, including the process and timeframe for delivery of their services. The objective of the OLA is to present a clear, concise, and measurable description of the service provider's internal support relationships. Before agreeing a major incident SLA period to resolve with the business it is essential that the operational-level agreements with all the major incident team members can support this SLA. For example, an SLA of four hours to resolve priority 1 incidents would be difficult to meet if the OLA to respond to a call out by a support group is 3 hours.

9.3   Underpinning Contracts (UC)

The underpinning contract is a contract between an IT service provider and a third party. The third party provides supporting services that enable the service provider to deliver a service to a customer. As is the case with OLA's the terms and conditions of underpinning contracts should reflect and be reflected in the appropriate SLAs.

Section 10: Major Incident Management Metrics

10 Major Incident Management Metrics

It is hard to define precise and descriptive metrics for the performance of major incident management. Major incident management performance must be measured against the objective which is reiterated here:

The purpose of the incident management process is to restore normal service operation as quickly as possible and minimize the adverse impact on business operations, ensuring that agreed levels of service quality are maintained.

With this purpose in mind, key performance indicators (KPIs) that will help evaluate the success of major incident management could include:

- Percentage of major incidents resolved within the agreed (SLA) time:
  This KPI measures performance against a primary objective of restoring normal service operation as quickly as possible.

- Percentage of major incidents reopened/repeated:
  This KPI measures performance against the quality of the resolution be it a fix or a workaround.

- Customer satisfaction scores: Service owners and business representatives could score major incident management on the quality of service provided.

Section 11:

Major Incident Management During the Incident

11 Major Incident Management During the Incident

Managing a major incident can be stressful. A Major Incident Manager needs to be strong, decisive, calm under pressure and authoritative enough to face senior management and customers in a hostile context. The most effective way of reducing stress while managing a major incident is preparation.

11.1 Major Incident Management Preparation

The most important action to ensure a Major Incident can be managed effectively and efficiently is preparation. To summarize the preparatory actions:

- Agree with the business what constitutes a major incident. Impacted stakeholders may encourage that the major incident management process be invoked for issues that are not necessarily major. With incidents being properly prioritised the major incident management process will not be overloaded.

- Ensure an up-to-date contact list, availability rota and escalation plan. Engaging the resolution teams and escalating when required is a crucial responsibility of a Major Incident Manager. Without these tools progress is delayed, and stress levels will rise.
- Have a structured and agreed communication plan in place. All stakeholders will know what communications they will receive and the frequency. When a major incident is declared there is momentous pressure to provide stakeholders, including customers, reliable updates.
- Have a structured and sequential major incident management process in place. This process is agreed with all stakeholders and ensures a consistent approach to managing all major incidents.
- Roles and responsibilities defined and agreed. There should be no debates around responsibilities during a major incident.

11.2 Managing a Major Incident

Management consists of controlling a group or a set of entities to accomplish a goal.

When managing a major incident, the Major Incident Manager will need to:

- Note all facts and symptoms.
- Establish any theories and hypothesis that may have caused the incident.
- Consider any workaround that would minimise the impact of the major incident.
- Establish action plans to progress to resolution of the incident.
- When scoping the major incident any discounted 'red herrings' should be noted to prevent resolution teams from circling back to them without any additional evidence.

11.2.1   The Start of a Major Incident

- Typical Challenges:
  - There may be hesitation to raise a major incident. A decision must be made.

- Little information is known:
  - There may be few symptoms
  - The severity of the symptoms (impact) might not be understood
  - The information available is often uncertain
- Only a few people may be working on the problem with limited stakeholder engagement
- Engineers working on the incident may not understand the impact.
- Responsibilities and ownership may not be defined

- Major Incident Checklist

At this challenging point it is useful to have a checklist to establish:
- Who is the Major Incident Manager?
- Are all the correct resolver teams working on the incident?
  - Need a list of names of subject matter experts

- Does third level support need to be engaged?
  - Understand the impact (current and potential)
  - Prioritise the symptoms
  - Management escalation
    - What management that needs to know?
    - When is the call with the impacted business?
    - Share the knowledge of the incident (symptoms, impact, technical information)
  - When did it start? Where there any recent changes to the system?
  - Any theories or hypothesis as to the cause of the incident?

A useful grid that will help a Major Incident Manager keep track could look like this:

Fact and Symptoms:	Theories:
• File x not received by system x • Server x CPU at 95%	• Alerting failure preventing CPU management • Potential network issue • Recent change to server
Action Plan:	**Red Herrings:**
• Add server space – Tom • Delay report submission to business – Fred • Check network health – Sarah • Check server alerting – John	• DBA confirmed no data issues with file

This helps the Major Incident Manager maintain control of the incident, manage the action plan, and provide consolidated updates on status to stakeholders.

11.2.2 Typically, the Second Hour of a Major Incident

- Typical Challenges:
  - Individual teams may work in silos
  - Operations guides may be overlooked
  - Obvious actions may typically be done after the first hour
  - Blame starts ("This is not my area – my checks are fine")

- Major Incident Manager Role:
  - Bring everyone together in a meeting
  - Have we contacted all the relevant third parties (suppliers, support contracts)?
  - Record the action plan
  - Do we have all the skills required? Are any escalations required?
  - Establish the facts – What is fake news (red herrings)
  - Can we reduce the impact (mitigations, workarounds)?
  - Review the diagram as a team – identify points of failure
  - Log reviews
  - Do know what is normal behaviour/ performance?
  - Is the information available to host a conference call with the business – Impact, symptoms, threads of investigation?

11.2.3 Typically, the Third Hour of a Major Incident

- Typical Challenges:
  - Investigative avenues are exhausted – the action list gets shorter
  - Blame continues ("I told you my checks are fine")
  - The team becomes tired and devoid of ideas

- Major Incident Manager Role:
  - Bring everyone together in a meeting
  - Is there a valid hypothesis?
  - What is the plan to validate/fix the hypothesis?
  - Review the action list
  - What is the nuclear option? What would fix the problem whatever the cost?
  - Consider looking after staff. Have they eaten?

Section 12:
Post Major Incident Review

12 Post Major Incident Review

A major incident review takes place after a major incident has occurred. The review documents the Incident's underlying causes (if known) and the complete resolution history and identifies opportunities for improving the handling of future major incidents.

This is an opportunity to capture any lessons learnt, update the knowledge base, and add actions to the continuous service improvement plan.

It is best practice to produce a major incident management review report within a service level agreement period. The following is only a simple example of a major incident review report's content as each organisation will have unique processes and circumstances.

- Succinct description of the incident
- Downtime duration
- SLA impact
- Short incident history
- How the incident was resolved
- What is the root cause?

- A set of activities scheduled in to prevent this kind of downtime

Where root cause remains unknown the problem management process is invoked to conduct the root cause analysis.

Section 13: Succeeding as a Major Incident Manager

13 Succeeding as a Major Incident Manager

13.1 Daily Challenges of a Major Incident Manager

A Major Incident Manager will face the following challenges:

- A key challenge of a Major Incident Manager is to deal with unknowns. Unless the Major Incident Manager is a subject matter expert the challenge is to competently lead the management of the major incident without this expertise. The Major Incident Manager will need to invoke the expertise of subject matter experts to competently lead the major incident to resolution.
- The scope in engagement for a major incident needs to consider people (e.g., subject matter experts) process (e.g., the existence of monitoring) and technology (e.g., software and hardware issue).
- With these challenges a high-quality service in a high-pressure environment needs to be delivered.

- Managing alpha personalities so ensure all stakeholders contribute to resolution.
- Managing a major incident can be stressful when unprepared. Even with preparation major incidents can be unique, and flexibility will inevitability be required.

13.2 Major Incident Leadership

Management consists of controlling a group or a set of entities to accomplish a goal. Everything covered in this book so far talks to the management of a major incident.

Leadership refers to an individual's ability to influence, motivate and enable others to contribute toward organisational success. Influence and inspiration separate leaders from managers, not power and control. A good leader has the courage to take appropriate risks. Relationships are built and influenced by the leader based on trust and loyalty. A good leader sees people as competent, acts as a change agent, always asks questions, and always looks for innovation and continuous improvement.

A Major Incident Manager will need to have all the tools to deliver resolutions and will need to consider a leadership style depending on the situation. There are three defined leadership styles:

13.2.1   Authoritarian Style

With this style leader makes decisions and instructs the team. Compliance is expected without feedback. This style can be invoked is highly urgent emergency situations where action is required immediately to resolve an incident.

13.2.2   Democratic Style

With this style the leader encourages idea sharing and contributions from everyone. The leader will also seek to ensure contributions are not dominated by Alpha personalities. The leader makes use of the expertise available but remains accountable for making the final decision. This style could be used when resolution is not urgent. There is time available that can be used to ensure the optimal resolution is defined.

13.2.3   Laissez-Faire

With this style the leader delegates decisions. Team members are empowered to make decisions. A Major Incident Manager may use this style where there are complex incidents requiring actions and decisions from multiple teams. Teams could be divided into autonomous groups with the necessary expertise and autonomy define and implement a resolution.

13.3 Conflict Management During a Major Incident

Conflicts are disagreements were the participants involved perceive a threat to their own needs, concerns, or values. Their own wellbeing is threatened be it emotional, physical, power or image. People tend to perceive a situation through their own lenses. Their perception is filtered through their lenses based on their own values, beliefs, life experience and even gender. Creative problem solving can turn conflict into opportunities for ideas and solutions. Understanding the five styles of conflict management will enable a Major Incident Manager to use them advantageously depending on the context and the relationship.

13.3.1   Accommodating Style

Ones values are given up in favour of the values of others. This option is about keeping the peace, not putting in more effort than the issue is worth and knowing when to pick battles. While it might seem weak, accommodation can be the absolute best choice to resolve a small conflict and move on with more critical issues. This style is highly cooperative on the part of the resolver but can lead to resentment.

13.3.2   Avoiding Style

Here the existence of the conflict is not recognised. It requires no courage nor consideration to address. This style aims to reduce conflict by ignoring it, removing the conflicted parties, or evading it. This can be an effective conflict resolution style if there is a chance that a cool-down period would be helpful or if you need more time to consider your stance on the conflict itself. Avoidance should not be a substitute for proper resolution, however; pushing back conflict indefinitely can and will lead to more (and bigger) conflicts down the line.

13.3.3   Competing Style

Here the objective is to win the battle. Ones values are upheld in favour of the values of others. This can be in situations where morals dictate that a specific course of action is taken, when there is no time to try and find a different solution or when there is an unpopular decision to be made. This style takes encourage, but it has consequences. There are short term advantages as your values prevail. If overused in the long term it will result in demotivation, disengagement, and distrust in a working relationship.

13.3.4　Compromising Style

This style seeks to find the middle ground by asking both parties to concede aspects of their desires so that a solution can be agreed upon. This style is sometimes known as lose-lose, in that both parties will have to give up a few things to agree on the larger issue. This is used when there is a time crunch, or when a solution simply needs to happen, rather than be perfect. This style is sometimes known as lose-lose, in that both parties will have to give up a few things to agree on the larger issue. This is used when there is a time This style is sometimes known as lose-lose, in that both parties will have to give up a few things to agree on the larger issue.

13.3.5　Collaboration Style

This style produces the best long-term results, at the same time it is often the most difficult and time-consuming to reach. Each party's needs and wants are considered, and a win-win solution is found so that everyone leaves satisfied. This often involves all parties sitting down together, talking through the conflict, and negotiating a solution together. This is used when it is vital to preserve the relationship between all parties or when the solution itself will have a significant impact. This style will most commonly be used in the post incident review following resolution of the major incident. At this stage it can also be useful to repair the damage to relationships caused by less collaborative styles necessarily used during the major incident.

13.3.6 Major Incident Management of Personality Types

A major incident manager would benefit from understanding the Myers Briggs defined personality types. The four categories are introversion / extraversion, sensing / intuition, thinking / feeling, judging / perceiving. According to the Myers Briggs, each person is said to have one preferred quality from each category, producing 16 unique types.

A major incident manager needs to ensure introverted team members opinions are heard.

Additionally, when the major incident team members are all a similar personality type 'group think' loses the benefit of diversity that multiple personality types could provide. In this situation the major incident manager needs to step out of his own personality type to add diversity to the team.

13.3.7 Approaching Major Incident Management Compassionately

To develop trust a Major Incident Manager needs to act with integrity and kindness before, during and after the incident. In doing so the Major Incident Manager becomes trusted.

The Major Incident Manager needs to be aware that those who are responsible for causing the major incident may feel awful and to progress constructively the Major Incident Manager needs to relieve them of this feeling.

The word 'blameless' should be avoided as it infers the issue is being hidden. The words 'post-mortem' should also be avoided as they infer that we are learning only from what went wrong and not ensuring the organisation benefits from the lessons learnt on what went well.

13.3.7.1   Organisational Compassion

For individuals to work compassionately it is helpful for the organisation to have compassionate traits:

- Helping people find a role that fits rather than managing people out
- Equally distributing the work and the credit rather than a hero culture
- Working together to develop shared priorities rather than on department drives everything
- Trusting employees with guardrails in place rather than sweeping policies

13.3.7.2 Major Incident Manager Compassion

The first tool of being compassionate is preparedness. Documents are up to date, your access if up to date, contact information readily available, company and team conventions for incident communication are known, major incident management and back up availability ensured.

During an incident, the Major Incident Manager will need to take breaks when needed to remain effective. Compassionate Major Incident Manager traits are:

- Communicates frequently. Asks for what is needed.
- Says please and thank you.
- Avoids accusatory language such as:
  - "Looks like you have the right people on board. How can I help?" rather than "Why did you page me?"
  - "Do we have someone available to roll back the change?" rather than "Who introduced the change?,"
  - "Is there something else we need to move forward?" rather than "Just fix it."
- Is cognizant of people's readiness levels considering the time of day, home life duties, breaks and check ins.

- Reaches out to colleagues who are stretched. Looks for ways to help but asks before acting.
- Keeps conversation appropriate. Stays on topic when trouble shooting is heated. Is careful with humour. Humour may not be appreciated by team members who are struggling or feel accountable.
- Let people know when you are taking time off to decompress.

To develop trust a Major Incident Manager needs to act with integrity and kindness before, during and after the incident. In doing so the Major Incident Manager becomes trusted.

The Major Incident Manager needs to be aware that those who are responsible for causing the major incident may feel awful and to progress constructively the Major Incident Manager needs to relieve them of this feeling.

The word 'blameless' should be avoided as it infers the issue is being hidden. The words 'post-mortem' should also be avoided as they infer that we are learning only from what went wrong and not ensuring the organisation benefits from the lessons learnt on what went well.

13.4 Critical Thinking for Major Incident Management

Sceptical, rational, and unbiased analysis of evidence to form a judgement is a vital skill of any major incident manager. Faulty logic and bias will delay resolution. A well cultivated thinker raises problems, articulates them well, gathers and accesses information, and is open minded.

A major incident manager needs to scrutinise arguments, which in this context is a reason that supports a theory, idea, or belief, for sound logic.

A simplistic example would be a major incident manager is engaged as it is reported by a user who cannot access a server that the server is down and therefore the entire environment is down. Evidence needs to be scrutinised to confirm that the server is in fact down and that it resulted in the entire environment being down.

Every major incident management participant will have conscious and unconscious biases that may influence the conclusions they make. All conclusions need to be evidence based.

13.5 Surviving as a Major Incident Manager

- Understanding if the major incident escalation is in fact a high priority incident or an opportunity to educate. Use an incident that has inappropriately been requested to be upgraded to a major incident as an opportunity to escalate and build the relationship.
- Know the defined roles and responsibilities of the Major Incident Manager and all other resolving participants.
- Know the KPI's which will measure performance.
- Understand the organisational processes both to understand the issues root cause and/or contributing factors and to ensure applicable processes are followed during the major incident. To establish that goal a standard template could be used with a list of top questions.
- Ideally a Major Incident Manager looks first to influence and then to persuade. Understand the

personality types and consider the best approach to engage and influence.

- A Major Incident Manager will always have the goal in mind and will keep the team focused on that goal.
- A Major Incident Manager will be a master of the tools available (see Section 5 for available tools). Using these tools should be second nature to a Major Incident Manager.
- Will always call out areas where opportunities for improvement are called out and logged.
- As well as taking care of the team do take care of yourself. You will need breaks, sleep, nutrition, and exercise.
- Learn from others. Observing and applying the techniques of organisationally respected colleagues. Partner with trusted teammates who can identify weak points.

13.5.1   A Word About Multi-Tasking

It is commonly quoted that a Major Incident Manager needs to be good at multi-tasking.

What multi-tasking is needs to be qualified? By example:

- You are writing an update to the major incident. While you are doing so a senior manager phones you with a question. You attempt to answer that question while continuing to write the update. This approach to multi-tasking is impossible and will lead to mistakes and a drop in the quality of the service you are providing.

- You are writing an update to the major incident. While you are doing so a senior manager phones you with a question. You decide on which of these tasks takes priority. You then either stop writing the update while answering the question or politely put the senior manager on hold explaining the priority.

The so-called multi-tasking skill is not one where you can conduct two tasks simultaneously but a skill to quickly transition from one interrupted task to the next. At any one time you are focused on a single task. This quick transition between interrupted tasks is the skill of multi-tasking.

Printed in Great Britain
by Amazon

26055853R00069